Princess Poppy's

· Cookbook ·

and Other Special Gifts to Make and Share

Janey Louise Jones

PICTURE CORGI

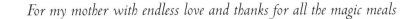

For my mother with endless love and thanks for all the magic meals

PRINCESS POPPY'S COOK BOOK: AND OTHER SPECIAL GIFTS TO MAKE AND SHARE
A PICTURE CORGI BOOK 978 1 849 41881 2

Published in Great Britain by Picture Corgi,
an imprint of Random House Children's Publishers UK
A Random House Group Company

This edition published 2013

1 3 5 7 9 10 8 6 4 2

Text copyright © Janey Louise Jones, 2007, 2013
Illustrations copyright © Random House Children's Publishers, 2013

The right of Janey Louise Jones to be identified as the author of this work has been asserted in accordance with the Copyright, Designs and Patents Act 1988.

Picture Corgi Books are published by Random House Children's Publishers UK,
61–63 Uxbridge Road, London W5 5SA

www.randomhousechildrens.co.uk
www.randomhouse.co.uk
www.princesspoppy.co.uk

Addresses for companies within The Random House Group Limited can be found at: www.randomhouse.co.uk/offices.htm

THE RANDOM HOUSE GROUP Limited Reg. No. 954009

A CIP catalogue record for this book is available from the British Library.

Printed in China

The Random House Group Limited supports the Forest Stewardship Council® (FSC®), the leading international forest certification organization. Our books carrying the FSC label are printed on FSC®-certified paper. FSC is the only forest certification scheme endorsed by the leading environmental organizations, including Greenpeace. Our paper procurement policy can be found at www.randomhouse.co.uk/environment.

MIX
Paper from
responsible sources
FSC® C104723

Contents

	Page
About This Book	4–5
Things You'll Need	6–7
PERFECT PRINCESS PARTY	8–9
Make a Princess Poppy Tiara	10–11
My Strawberry Cream Sponge Cake	12–13
Bunting Decoration	14–15
Rocky Road Cakes	16–17
Daisy's Fruity Banana Split	18–19
Mimosa's Muffins	20–21
PRINCESS PICNIC	22–23
Aunt Marigold's Cloudy Lemonade	24
Poppy's Favourite Cucumber Sandwiches	25
Mum's Sticky Cocktail Sausages	26–27
Saffron's Mini Quiches	28–29
Sweetpea's Petal Cakes	30–31
Flower Pressing with Princess Poppy	32–33
Friendship Bracelets with Princess Poppy and Honey	34–35
WINTER WONDERLAND	36–37
Granny Bumble's Biscuits	38–39
Christmas Cards	40–41
Mrs Meadowsweet's Comfort Cottage Pie	42–43
Make Your Own Christmas Stocking	44–45
Carrot and Potato Soup	46–47
Holly's Chocolate Hedgehogs	48–49
Gift Box	50–51
SPARKLING SPRING	52–53
Grandpa's Brilliant Bread	54–55
Poppy's Penne Pasta	56–57
Peach, Chicken and Herb Salad	58–59
Aunt Delphi's Pear and Chocolate Crumble	60–61
Easy Lavender Bag	62–63

About This Book

This gorgeous book is designed to get you cooking and crafting with Princess Poppy. Whether you are new to cooking and baking or have practised with a grown-up before, then we hope you will find some new food ideas to try. Why not have a Princess Party with cakes and princess tiaras? Or have a lovely picnic (you can have it indoors if it's raining outside!) with fresh bread, quiches and cloudy lemonade? There's plenty of activities for you to try!

Weighing and Measuring

This is an important part of making sure the recipes come out as they are supposed to, so check you have the right amount of ingredients before you start. You can use scales, measuring jugs or measuring spoons for this.

Cooking Times

Each recipe has an oven temperature and cooking time to help make sure your recipe is cooked enough. Ask a grown-up what kind of oven you have, and that will tell you what temperature you need to use. Don't forget to set a timer when things are in the oven!

These recipes are for the family to enjoy making together. Some could be dangerous without the help of an adult. Children, please have an adult with you when you are using knives, handling anything hot or using the food processor.

Getting Started

There are a few things you should know before you start...

IMPORTANT INFORMATION BEFORE YOU BEGIN!

★ Always have a grown-up to help you, even if you have cooked a recipe or done an activity before

★ The oven and hob are HOT: be careful when taking things out of, or putting things into the oven

★ Use oven-safe dishes, and make sure you put them on a heat-proof surface when they are taken out of the oven

★ Always wash your hands before cooking

★ Read the recipe through before you start

★ Keep the kitchen clean and make sure you tidy up as you go along

★ All portions and servings sizes are approximate

★ All recipes serve four people unless otherwise stated

★ Cooking is all about having fun! Don't worry if it doesn't work out first time – try again!

Things You'll Need

Here is a list of the basic things you will need for the recipes and crafts.

For the baking/cooking...

★ Measuring scales

★ Sieve

★ Mixing bowls

★ Assortment of wooden and metal spoons

★ Muffin and cake cases

★ Saucepans – varying sizes

★ Frying pan

★ Fork or whisk

★ Cake tins – various sizes are recommended in this book

★ Greaseproof paper and baking paper

★ Heat-proof dishes to go in the oven
(check with your parent or guardian which ones you should use)

★ Chopping board and knife
(with adult supervision)

★ Cheese grater

★ Cooling rack

★ Rolling pin

★ Serving dishes

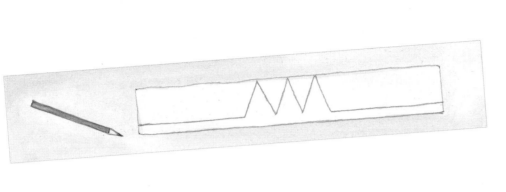

For the craft activities...

★ Card and paper
★ Pencil
★ Ruler
★ Glue and sticky tape
★ Tracing paper
★ Felt, scraps of fabric
★ Scissors
★ Cotton tape or ribbons
★ Needle and thread, or sewing machine, or strong staples

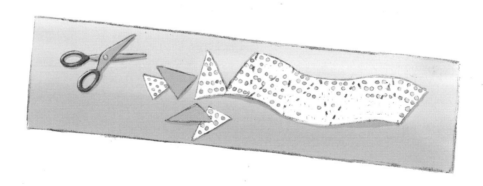

"Birthday parties are so special! Mum and Dad always make me feel like a princess on my birthday. Being a princess is about being kind and thoughtful, but it is nice to wear a tiara just to remind everyone! Honey and I love to help Mum make pretty bunting for parties, and it's great when you get to eat special treats like delicious Rocky Road, Fruity Banana Splits or Mimosa's Muffins!"

Perfect Princess Party

Make a Princess Poppy Tiara

"I know being a princess is on the inside, but I do so love wearing pretty princess things, especially tiaras!"

You will need

❖ A tape measure
❖ A long piece of card – long enough to fit around your head plus 2cm; gold or silver card looks really special
❖ Scissors, glue, a stapler or sticky tape
❖ Glitter glue, stickers, coloured pens or pencils to decorate your tiara
❖ Small squares of coloured tissue paper

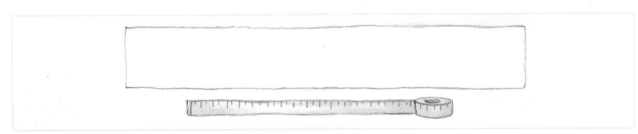

1. Cut a long piece of card to the correct length.

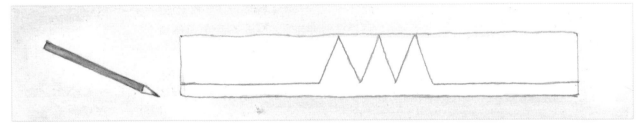

2. Draw a tiara shape onto the long piece of card, as shown.

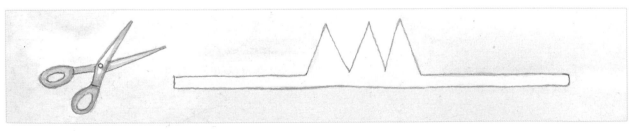

3. Cut it out.

4. Now decorate your tiara with glitter glue, stickers, pens or pencils – or even all of these things!

5. Make flowers from the tissue paper – pinch the middle point of the squares and gather in folds, as shown. They will look just like flower heads!

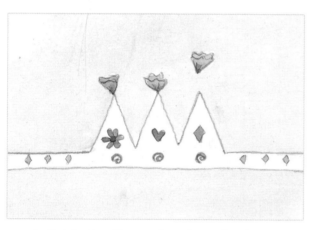

6. Stick the flower heads with glue onto each of the points and you'll have a tiara just like Poppy's.

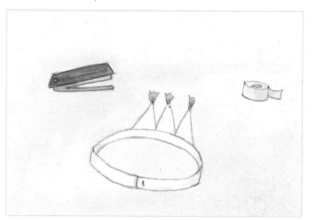

7. Leave everything to dry for 20–30 minutes, then fix the ends of the tiara together with sticky tape or a stapler. Make sure your tiara fits your head first!

"We're perfect princesses now!"

My Strawberry Cream Sponge Cake

"Granny Bumble made this for my surprise birthday party. Everyone thought it was DEEEELICIOUS!"

Ingredients

- ❖ 225g butter
- ❖ 225g caster sugar
- ❖ 2 eggs, beaten
- ❖ 2 teaspoons vanilla extract
- ❖ 225g self-raising flour
- ❖ Approx 2 tablespoons milk
- ❖ Strawberry jam
- ❖ Whipped cream
- ❖ White chocolate pieces
- ❖ Chopped strawberries
- ❖ Icing sugar

serves 6–8
★
takes
35 minutes

Utensils

- ❖ 2 x 20cm cake tins
- ❖ Baking paper
- ❖ Mixing bowl
- ❖ Metal spoon
- ❖ Wooden spoon
- ❖ Serving plate
- ❖ Sieve

What to do now

1. Preheat oven to 190°C/375°F/gas mark 5 and butter two 20cm cake tins and line with baking paper.

2. In a mixing bowl, cream the butter and sugar together, then add eggs and vanilla extract.

3. Fold in the flour with a metal spoon and add a little of the milk for smoothness, until you have a smooth, soft mixture.

4. Divide the mixture between the two tins, smooth the surface with a spatula or the back of a spoon. Pop in the oven to bake for 20 minutes until golden and bouncy to the touch. Turn out onto a cooling rack and allow to cool totally.

5. Spread the top of one sponge with strawberry jam and cover with whipped cream. You can add white chocolate pieces to the cream to make it even tastier!

6. Place a layer of chopped strawberries over the cream and sandwich the remaining sponge on top.

7. Sprinkle icing sugar through a sieve on the top of the cake to make it really magical.

Alternatively, add more cream and strawberries to the top for a gateau effect.

Bunting Decoration

"Making bunting is fun and really makes you feel ready to celebrate!"

You will need

❖ Card
❖ Scraps of fabric – old clothes, curtains, unwanted bedding or you can use strong paper if you don't have fabric
❖ Cotton tape or ribbons
❖ Needle and thread, or sewing machine, or strong staples

What to do now

1. Make a triangle template from card and cut out.

2. Make sure your piece of fabric is flat, then place your template over it. Cut the piece of fabric into triangles using the template.

3. Once you have cut a few pieces out you can attach to tape or ribbon at regular intervals, by stitching or stapling to make a nice pattern.

4. Hang up in the garden or indoors for an instant party feel!

Rocky Road Cakes

"Honey and I like making this for everyone to share!"

Ingredients

- ❖ 115g butter
- ❖ 1 tablespoon golden syrup
- ❖ 2 dessertspoons drinking chocolate
- ❖ 225g crushed digestive biscuits – crush in a bag with a rolling pin
- ❖ 1–2 drops vanilla essence
- ❖ Big bar of chocolate for melting over mixture

Goody suggestions:
handful of sultanas, cherries, marshmallows or Maltesers
– you choose!

Utensils

- ❖ 2 saucepans
- ❖ Swiss roll tin or shallow baking tin
- ❖ Wooden spoons
- ❖ Heatproof bowl for melting chocolate
- ❖ Rolling pin

makes
6–10 pieces
multiply to suit
★
takes
2 hours

What to do now

1. Melt the butter in a pan, then add the golden syrup. You can then add the drinking chocolate, crushed digestive biscuits and vanilla essence.

2. Add the 'goodies' of your choice.

3. Press the mixture into the Swiss roll tin and put in the fridge to chill.

4. While the cake is chilling, break the bar of chocolate into smallish pieces and put into a heatproof bowl. Put this over a pan of simmering water until chocolate is melted.

5. Take the cake out of the fridge, spread the melted chocolate over it (be careful – it will be hot) and put back in the fridge until the chocolate has set (gone hard).

6. Take the cake out of the fridge and cut it into squares, rectangles or triangles.

Daisy's Fruity Banana Split

"Cousin Daisy learned how to make this at the Lighthouse Café in Camomile Cove. It's such a treat when she makes it for us!"

Ingredients

❖ 1 large banana
❖ Oranges/strawberries/raspberries/ melon/peaches – as much as you like
❖ Ice cream – several flavours, if you want
❖ Whipped cream
❖ Chocolate sauce, nuts, chocolate flake, toffee or chocolate pieces to decorate

Utensils

❖ Long dessert dish or plate (or you can use a bowl)
❖ Chopping board
❖ Ice-cream scoop or spoon

ingredients are for 1 split– multiply to suit
★
takes 3–5 minutes per split

What to do now

1. Slice the banana in half lengthways and chop the other fruit into small pieces.

2. Arrange the banana and other fruit in the dish or bowl.

3. Add three scoops of ice cream in between the banana halves.

4. Swirl a little whipped cream on top of each scoop of ice cream.

5. Decorate with chocolate sauce, chocolate pieces, nuts or toffee pieces. Yummy!

Mimosa's Muffins

"My friend Mimosa loves to gather apples from the big apple tree in the grounds of the Hedgerows Hotel where she lives. Try her delicious apple and vanilla muffins."

Ingredients

❖ 75g butter
❖ 100g golden caster sugar
❖ 225g plain flour, mixed with 3 teaspoons of baking powder
❖ 225ml buttermilk or milk
❖ 100g peeled and chopped apples
❖ Seeds from a vanilla pod, or a dash of vanilla extract

Utensils

❖ Muffin tin (with at least 8 wells)
❖ Muffin cases
❖ Mixing bowl
❖ Sieve
❖ Cooling rack
❖ Serving plate

makes 8
★
takes
40 minutes

What to do now

1. Preheat the oven to 200°C/400°F/ gas mark 6.
2. Line the wells of a muffin tin with muffin cases.

3. In a mixing bowl cream the butter and sugar, then sieve the flour and baking powder in and stir in the buttermilk.

4. Fold the apples and the vanilla into the mixture.

5. Divide between the cases and put these in the oven for 25 minutes until golden.

6. Cool on a wire rack and get ready to eat these yummy treats.

"Picnics are such good fun for all the family! All the grown-ups are relaxed, we play games and the food is super-scrummy. I love to help Granny Bumble with picnic food and drinks. We take Aunt Marigold's Cloudy Lemonade and Cucumber Sandwiches – yum! Oh, and Mum makes these Sticky Sausages – if you think normal sausages are good, wait until you taste these! Saffron usually brings amazing Mini Quiches, and Sweetpea does the cutest ever Petal Cakes! Afterwards, Honey and I love to press flowers and make friendship bracelets."

Princess Picnic!

Aunt Marigold's Cloudy Lemonade

You will need
❖ 6 tablespoons caster sugar
❖ Water (1½–3 litres)
❖ 6 fresh lemons
❖ A jug

makes 1 jug
★
takes
20 minutes

What to do

1. Boil the sugar and water — then leave syrup to cool.

2. Juice the lemons.

3. Mix the lemon juice and the sugar/water syrup together in a jug.

4. Dilute with water until it tastes just right.

Poppy's Favourite Cucumber Sandwiches

You will need
❖ Sliced bread – white or brown, whichever you like best
❖ Butter
❖ Cucumber

makes
2 sandwiches
★
takes
10 minutes

What to do

1. Butter the bread.

2. Cut a cucumber into thin slices.

3. Lay the sliced cucumber on the bread, slightly away from the crusts, then put the top piece of bread on, butter-side down.

4. Remove the crusts and cut the sandwiches into dainty triangles.

Mum's Sticky Cocktail Sausages

"Mum makes these for birthday parties, picnics, and as a special treat on Saturday nights! Yum!"

Ingredients
❖ 20 cocktail sausages or 10 sausages cut in half
❖ 2 tablespoons dark soy sauce (lower salt variety if possible)
❖ 2 tablespoons runny honey, ideally in a squeezy drizzle-style bottle

Utensils
❖ A large roasting pan
❖ A cup for mixing the glaze
❖ A brush for coating the sausages with the glaze (optional)

serves 6–10
along with other party nibbles
★
takes
30 minutes

What to do now

1. Preheat the oven to 180°C/350°F/ gas mark 4.

2. Spread the sausages evenly in the roasting tin.

3. Pop it in the oven to roast for 15 minutes.

4. Mix the soy sauce and honey in a cup to form a glaze.

5. Remove the sausages from the oven and cover with glaze, using brush. Be careful – they'll be hot!

6. Roast for a further 15 minutes until golden, sticky and cooked through.

Saffron's Mini Quiches

"These are so easy to eat at picnics and parties. And so yummy too!"

Ingredients
- ❖ A drop of vegetable oil for frying
- ❖ 1 onion, finely diced
- ❖ Your choice of chopped courgette, tomatoes, bacon, mushrooms
- ❖ 6 eggs, beaten
- ❖ 1 cup cream
- ❖ 1 cup grated cheese
- ❖ Salt and pepper
- ❖ 1 kg ready-rolled shortcrust pastry (6 sheets)

Utensils
- ❖ Small frying pan
- ❖ Chopping board
- ❖ Mini muffin tray (12 wells)
- ❖ Spoons
- ❖ Glass or cup for cutting circles of pastry

makes 12
★
takes
30 minutes

What to do now

1. Preheat the oven to 180°C/350°F/ gas mark 4.

2. Fry the onion with the other filling ingredients of your choice over a low heat until soft and cooked through.

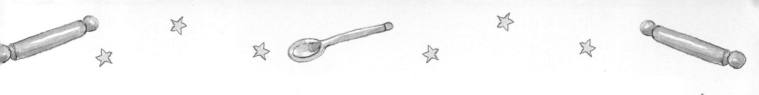

3. Allow to cool a little, then mix with the eggs, cream, cheese and seasoning.

4. Lay out the sheets of pastry, then, using a glass or cup, cut 12 circles.

5. Lightly oil the muffin tray with butter or oil and press the circles of pastry into the wells.

6. Place two spoonfuls of the mixture into each pastry base.

7. Bake for 10–12 minutes until golden and set. (Repeat if you have leftover pastry and filling.)

Sweetpea's Petal Cakes

"These cakes are very special. Sweetpea just loves to make pretty cakes!"

Ingredients

- ❖ 110g soft butter
- ❖ 110g caster sugar
- ❖ 2 free-range eggs, lightly beaten
- ❖ 1 teaspoon vanilla extract
- ❖ 110g self-raising flour, sieved
- ❖ 1–2 tablespoons milk

For the icing:
- ❖ 300g icing sugar
- ❖ 2–3 tablespoons water
- ❖ 2–3 drops food colouring
(you can pick the colour!)

Utensils

- ❖ 2 x fairy cake tins (12 well)
- ❖ Fairy cake cases
- ❖ Mixing bowl
- ❖ Cooling rack

For the petals:
- ❖ 150g white sugar paste

makes 24
★
takes
35 minutes

What to do now

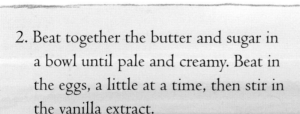

1. Preheat the oven to 180°C/350°F/ gas mark 4 and place paper cases in 2 x 12–well fairy cake tins.

2. Beat together the butter and sugar in a bowl until pale and creamy. Beat in the eggs, a little at a time, then stir in the vanilla extract.

3. Fold in the flour using a large metal spoon. Add a little milk until the mixture is a soft dropping consistency, and now spoon the mixture into the paper cases until they are half full.

4. Bake in the oven for 8–10 minutes, or until golden-brown on top and a skewer inserted into one of the cakes comes out clean. Set aside to cool for 10 minutes, then remove from the tin and cool on a wire rack.

For the icing:

1. Sieve the icing sugar into a large mixing bowl and stir in enough water to create a smooth mixture. Stir in the food colouring, and spread a little on top of each cake.

2. To decorate, make petals by dusting a board with icing sugar, then colour the sugar paste pink and roll it out to form petals of around ½cm.

Flower Pressing
with Princess Poppy

You will need

❖ A selection of your favourite flowers – Poppy's favourites are pansies, roses, tulips, daisies – and poppies, of course

❖ A flower press or some big heavy books – try a dictionary or an encyclopaedia

❖ A roll of Kitchen paper

❖ Card, sticky-back plastic, glue, and gold or silver pens

"I want my favourite flowers to live for ever, so Grandpa showed me a way to do this. Every year we press lots of flowers and make cards and pictures out of them – it's easy and fun!"

I. Pick some flowers from the garden – always ask a grown-up first. Do not pick them after it has rained, as they must be dry.

2. Open the book near the back, lay some kitchen paper on the page, then put the flowers you want to press on the kitchen paper.

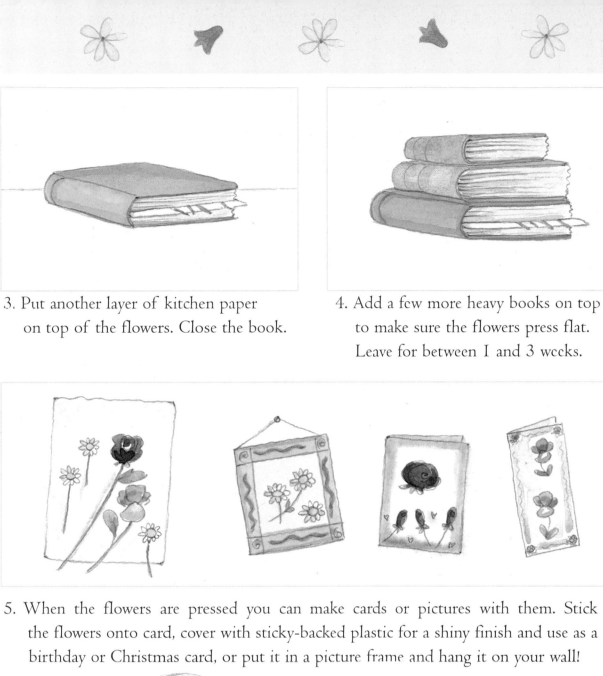

3. Put another layer of kitchen paper on top of the flowers. Close the book.

4. Add a few more heavy books on top to make sure the flowers press flat. Leave for between 1 and 3 weeks.

5. When the flowers are pressed you can make cards or pictures with them. Stick the flowers onto card, cover with sticky-backed plastic for a shiny finish and use as a birthday or Christmas card, or put it in a picture frame and hang it on your wall!

"My pressed-flower picture will look really pretty on my bedroom wall!"

Friendship Bracelets with Princess Poppy and Honey

You will need

❖ Long, strong, thick thread in all your favourite colours – about 18cm long

❖ 1 piece of paper

❖ Sticky tape

"Me and Honey have been best friends for ever so one day we decided to make friendship bracelets for each other. You can make them for your best friend too – it's easy!"

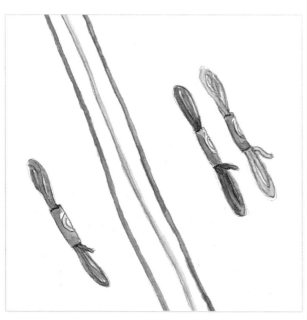

1. Choose 3 strands of different coloured thread – make sure they look nice together.

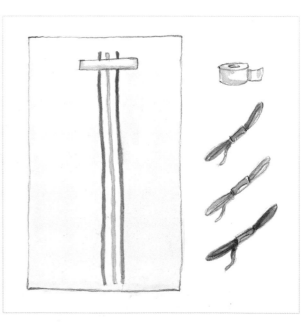

2. Stick one end of each thread onto the paper, as shown.

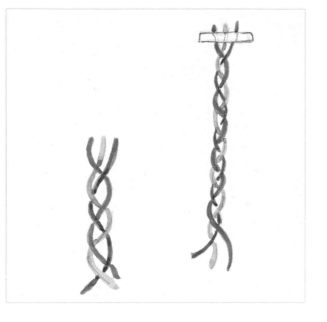

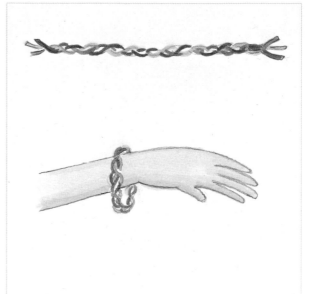

3. Now plait the threads.

4. When the bracelet is long enough, take it off the paper and ask a grown-up to help you tie a knot in both ends and then fasten it around your wrist.

"Me and Honey have matching friendship bracelets to show that we're the best of friends!"

Winter Wonderland

"Winter is probably my absolute favourite time of year, because you can play in the snow then get all cosy and snuggly indoors. We love sipping hot chocolate with Granny Bumble's Biscuits by the log fire. And Mum often makes us her yummy Carrot and Potato Soup. At Christmas time I usually make presents, such as Holly's Chocolate Hedgehogs, or gift boxes. Or even a Christmas stocking! Honey and I like to make our own Christmas cards too. Friends and family love it when you make an effort."

Granny Bumble's Biscuits

"Granny Bumble is the best biscuit maker in the whole world. She makes these scrummy biscuits for Bumble's Teashop."

Ingredients

- ❖ 100g soft unsalted butter
- ❖ 100g caster sugar
- ❖ 1 free-range egg, lightly beaten
- ❖ 1 teaspoon vanilla extract
- ❖ 275g plain flour

For the icing:

- ❖ 400g icing sugar
- ❖ 3–4 tablespoons water
- ❖ A few drops food colouring

Utensils

- ❖ Baking tray
- ❖ Greaseproof paper
- ❖ Mixing bowl
- ❖ Spoons
- ❖ Rolling pin
- ❖ Biscuit cutters
- ❖ Cooling rack

makes 6–8
★
takes
30 minutes

What to do now

1. Preheat the oven to 190°C/375°F/ gas mark 5.
2. Line a baking tray with greaseproof paper.
3. Cream butter and sugar in a bowl until combined and smooth.

4. Beat in the egg and vanilla little by little.

5. Stir in the flour until the mixture forms a dough, then roll out using a rolling pin.

6. Using biscuit cutters, cut the biscuits out of the dough and place on the baking tray – these can be any shape you like.

7. Bake biscuits for 8–10 minutes. Cool on a wire rack.

8. Sieve the icing sugar into a bowl and mix with enough water to form a thin paste, then add drops of food colouring ready to start decorating.

Spread a little icing on top of each biscuit, and decorate with icing flowers, tiny edible silver balls or edible jewels!

Christmas Cards

"Honey and I made Christmas cards using bits and pieces from our craft box. This is just one idea. You can have fun trying out different combinations!"

You will need

- ❖ Plain folded cards or sheets of card which you can fold
- ❖ Pretty wrapping paper or wallpaper
- ❖ Glue
- ❖ Scissors
- ❖ Scraps of felt
- ❖ Ribbons
- ❖ Small silver balls or bells or snowflake shapes or glitter (optional)

What to do now

1. Cover the front of the card by gluing on pretty paper as a background.

2. Cut a square of light-coloured felt as a backdrop to the tree.

3. Cut out a Christmas tree from green felt. You can stick on 'baubles' cut from felt or use silver baubles.

4. Add a red bow to the top of the tree and stick to the front of the card.

5. Decorate as you wish, with writing, glitter, balls or snowflakes.

Mrs Meadowsweet's Comfort Cottage Pie

"This dish is easy to make, easy to eat and easy to love. It's perfect on cold days, and the twins love it too."

Ingredients

- ❖ 3 tablespoons olive oil
- ❖ 1¼ kg lean beef mince
- ❖ 2 onions, chopped
- ❖ 3 tablespoons plain flour
- ❖ 1 tablespoon tomato purée
- ❖ 850ml beef stock
- ❖ Seasoning
- ❖ 4 teaspoons Worcester sauce

For the mash:
- ❖ 1.8kg potatoes, peeled and chopped into small pieces
- ❖ 225ml milk
- ❖ 30g butter
- ❖ 200g grated cheese
- ❖ Seasoning and nutmeg (optional)

Utensils

- ❖ Large frying pan
- ❖ Ovenproof serving dish
- ❖ Pan
- ❖ Chopping board
- ❖ Cheese grater

serves 4–6

★

takes

2 hours

What to do now

1. Heat half the oil in large pan and fry mince until brown, then put aside to rest.

2. Put the rest of the oil in the pan and add the onion. Soften on a gentle heat for around 15 minutes.

3. Add the flour and tomato purée and cook for a few minutes, then return the mince to the pan and add the beef stock.

4. Season and add Worcester
   sauce. Simmer for 45 minutes.
   Then preheat oven to
   180°C/350°F/gas mark 4.

5. Boil potatoes until tender. Drain
   and ensure they are very dry. Mash
   well with milk, butter and most of
   the cheese. Season to taste.

6. Spoon meat into an overproof
   dish and cover with mash.
   Sprinkle with remaining cheese
   and cook in the oven for 25–30
   minutes.

Make your Own Christmas Stocking

You will need

- ❖ A felt-tip pen
- ❖ Tracing paper
- ❖ Scissors
- ❖ 2 pieces of felt (stockings can be any size: tiny for tree decorations, or big for Father Christmas to put gifts in – for big ones, each piece of felt must be 42 x 30cm)
- ❖ Pins
- ❖ A large-eyed needle and thick thread
- ❖ Bright felt scraps
- ❖ Glue
- ❖ Sticky tape
- ❖ Sequins, beads, sparkly buttons, glitter glue – you choose!

Making the pattern

Draw a stocking shape on the tracing paper, cut it out. This is your pattern.

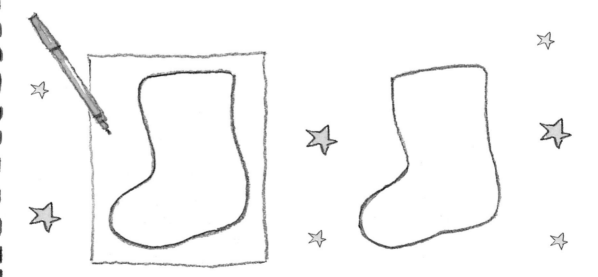

1. Lay the two pieces of felt on top of each other, pin the pattern onto the felt to cut around it.
2. Take the pattern off the felt.

3. Pin the 2 pieces of felt together Stitch around the edges, as shown (right).

4. Be as neat as you can and don't forget to leave the top open!
Stitch a loop of thread to the top of the stocking, so you can hang it up.
TIP: Start and finish the stitching with knots and hide the ends inside the stocking!

How to decorate your stocking

5. Draw small shapes onto tracing paper, pin onto felt scraps and cut them out.

6. Glue or stitch the felt shapes onto your stocking.
7. To make it look really special, glue sequins on, sew on beads, or even write your name on it with glitter glue!

Now all you need is Father Christmas!

Carrot and Potato Soup

"Perfect on colder days! This is my favourite soup EVER! And mum says it is very good for us!"

Ingredients

- ❖ 4 large potatoes
- ❖ 6 medium carrots
- ❖ 2 teaspoons of butter or oil
- ❖ 1 small onion, peeled and sliced
- ❖ 578ml vegetable stock
- ❖ Salt and pepper
- ❖ Pinch of mixed herbs

Utensils

- ❖ Chopping board
- ❖ Vegetable knife
- ❖ Grater (optional—you can either grate or chop carrots)
- ❖ Saucepan
- ❖ Wooden spoon

serves 4–6
★
takes
30 minutes

What to do now

1. Peel and dice potatoes into 1cm cubes.

2. Peel and chop carrots to the same size as before, or alternatively grate them.

3. Add the butter or oil to a pan then add onions and soften gently.

4. Pour in the stock and add carrots and potatoes, along with herbs and seasoning.

5. Simmer until potatoes are soft and fluffy and it's ready to eat!

Watch out — it might be hot!

Holly's Chocolate Hedgehogs

"My teacher, Holly Mallow, makes these at Christmas as an end-of-term treat. We'll do anything for one of her chocolate hedgehogs. The truffle mixture is scrumptious and they're so cute! Honey and I begged her for the recipe. And here it is!"

Ingredients

❖ 20 digestive biscuits
❖ 125g butter
❖ 200g condensed milk
❖ 2 tablespoons cocoa

For decoration:
❖ Chocolate strands
❖ Desiccated coconut
❖ Tiny chocolate balls

Utensils

❖ Plastic bags
❖ Rolling pin
❖ Saucepan
❖ Wooden spoon

makes 6
★
takes
25 minutes

What to do now

1. Put biscuits into a plastic bag and bash with a rolling pin, to make crumbs.

2. Put the butter and condensed milk in a pan over a low heat until butter melts. Leave to cool.

3. Add the biscuits and cocoa powder to the melted butter mix and stir well.

4. When the mixture has cooled enough, form into oval shapes by rolling with your hands.

5. Make a pointy hedgehog nose with your fingers.

6. Add the eyes and nose, then decorate the "back" of the hedgehog with either chocolate strands or coconut.

Yummy!

Gift Box

"This gorgeous gift box is perfect for putting presents in!"

You will need

❖ An empty chocolate box – the bigger the better and it must have an insert tray

❖ Gold paint and a paint brush

❖ Scissors and glue

❖ Some fabric – enough to line the inside of the box. Red velvet looks super gorgeous, but you can use any fabric scraps you have around the house

❖ Stickers, sequins, beads, glitter glue or stick-on jewels

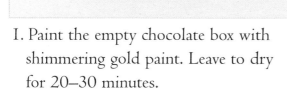

1. Paint the empty chocolate box with shimmering gold paint. Leave to dry for 20–30 minutes.

2. When the paint is dry, line the inside of the box by gluing the fabric and sticking it in place.

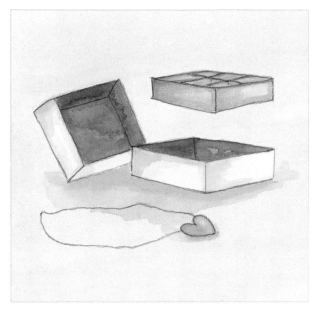

3. Lay the insert tray inside the box –
   this will help you keep your presents
   cosy.

4. Decorate the outside of your box
   with stickers, sequins, glitter glue,
   beads or stick-on jewels.

Sparkling Spring

"It's such fun when spring arrives in Honeypot Hill after a long, snowy winter. I love the brightly-coloured flowers in Sally's Lavender Garden Centre, and all the baby animals on Barley Farm. Honey and I also love to pick lavender and make sweet, scented bags with it. We get so hungry and it's great to help Mum and Grandpa with yummy snacks and meals. Grandpa and I make brilliant bread, which is so much nicer than the bread you get in the shops. I made up the perfect pasta recipe and also a peachy salad which everyone LOVES. In springtime, we go to Cousin Daisy's more and Aunt Delphi makes Pear and Chocolate Crunchy Crumble which is easily the best pudding in the WORLD!"

Poppy's Penne Pasta

"This is my favourite pasta dish and I always help Mum to make it when she's busy!"

Ingredients
- ❖ 400g of penne pasta
- ❖ Pinch of salt
- ❖ 2 tablespoons olive oil
- ❖ 3 rashers bacon
- ❖ 1 onion peeled and chopped (optional)
- ❖ Tin chopped tomatoes
- ❖ 2 large squirts of tomato purée
- ❖ Bay leaf (optional)
- ❖ 2 tablespoons peas
- ❖ Parmesan cheese, grated or shaved

Utensils
- ❖ Saucepan
- ❖ Frying pan
- ❖ Chopping board
- ❖ Serving dish

serves 4
★
takes
30 minutes

Why not add courgette instead of bacon as a vegetarian alternative!

What to do now

1. Boil the pasta for 15–20 minutes with a little salt until tender, but not too soft.

2. Grill or fry the bacon (or courgette) and chop into small pieces.

3. Heat the oil in frying pan and fry onion gently until see-through, add chopped tomatoes and tomato purée, plus salt, pepper and bay leaf (if you like). Simmer for 10–20 minutes.

4. Add bacon and peas to tomato sauce mix.

5. Drain pasta and add sauce, covering pasta evenly. Don't forget to take the bay leaf out before serving.

Yum!

6. Place in serving bowl and sprinkle with parmesan.

Easy Lavender Bag

You will need

❖ Dried or fresh lavender –
   I handful for each lavender bag

❖ A roll of kitchen paper

❖ Dried or fresh lavender –
   I handful for each lavender bag

❖ A square piece of muslin or
   gauze 30x30cm

❖ I rubber band for each lavender bag

❖ 30cm of pretty ribbon (per bag) –
   purple would look gorgeous

*"Last week
Granny Bumble
took me to the Lavender
Lake Garden Centre. We
bought some lavender
and later on she showed
me how to make
lavender bags."*

I. Cut some lavender if you have it in
your garden, if not, just buy some.

2. Rub off the flower heads onto kitchen
paper and if fresh lavender, leave to dry
out somewhere warm for about a week.

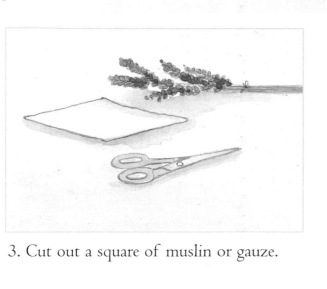

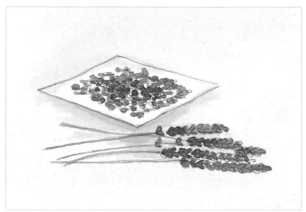

3. Cut out a square of muslin or gauze.

4. Place the dried lavender on the middle of the square.

5. Carefully gather up the edges – try not to spill any lavender! Fasten at the top with a rubber band, as shown.

6. Tie the ribbon around the band, making sure you cover the band completely.

"Hang lavender bags around the house or put them in your wardrobe to make your clothes smell really gorgeous! They are lovely, sweet-smelling presents – perfect for Mother's Day!"